THIS JOURNAL NOTEBOOK BELONGS TO: